OLD OTSEGO COUNTY
IN POSTCARDS

OLD OTSEGO COUNTY
IN POSTCARDS

David O'Connor

molly yes press

RD 3, BOX 70B
NEW BERLIN, NY 13411

Printed in the United States of America

Printing Number:
 2 3 4 5 6 7 8 9
19   83 84 85 86 87 88 89

ISBN 0-931308-11-9

MOLLY YES PRESS
RD 3, Box 70B
New Berlin, NY 13411

Contents

the place is mentioned, or a general fact of old-time life is related. The aim of these commentaries is to present information
regarding the past that might interest the reader.

The whole of America's history is mirrored in the history
of this county. It started with the Indians. We had Dutch, French,
German, and English residents before the Revolution. During
that conflict, armies of both sides marched across our land.
After the peace treaty was signed, Otsego's citizens fought to
shape a concept of democracy that is still being shaped today.
Otsego grew with the country. Our people fought wars, built
farms, schools, churches, factories, railroads, and highways.
When American literature blossomed, Otsego writers interpreted
the soul of the country. When the inventive spirit took hold, Otsego natives invented. Ambitious persons made fortunes here,
and when working men banded together to wrestle power from
them, union battles were fought on Otsego soil.

It is my hope that this book may both entertain and inspire

the reader to appreciate both the achievements of Otsego County's people and the human story of their daily lives. In short, I hope it does what good books should, namely, open the eyes of the reader a little wider so that significance will be seen in what before was passed unnoticed.

* * * * * * * * * *

I wish to acknowledge the help and support of my best friend and wife, Virginia O'Connor, in all stages of producing this book. Any original material herein is dedicated with love to her.

Pecktown Store Road, Pittsfield   David O'Connor
November, 1982

Cooperstown and Otsego Lake

E 1897 BIRD'S EYE VIEW OF COOPERSTOWN, N.Y.

BIRDSEYE VIEW OF COOPERSTOWN

It was such a view as this of Cooperstown and Otsego Lake that first inspired James Fenimore Cooper to begin the "Leatherstocking Tales." His daughter Susan claims that they were once riding together in a wagon heading home along the east side of the lake when he suddenly halted the wagon at a spot where the woods opened to reveal a view of the lake. After a moment of studying the scene in silence, he turned to his daughter and said, "I must write one more book, dearie, about our little lake!"

Soon after, he shut himself up in the library of Otsego Hall and produced "The Deerslayer," his first Leatherstocking novel.

"COUNCIL ROCK", OTSEGO LAKE, COOPERSTOWN, N. Y.   47

60035

COUNCIL ROCK

The first Europeans to ever visit Otsego County were a small party of Dutch explorers who scouted the area in the seventeenth century to determine its potential for fur trading. If the group encountered any Indians, they would probably have been of the Iroquois Nation, a newly formed confederacy of eight tribes who had recently chased out another people, the Algonquins, whose ancesters had lived in the area for thousands of years.

The two Iroquois tribes that inhabited Otsego County were the Mohawks, in the eastern part, and the Oneidas, in the rest of the county.

The Source of the Susquehanna River which rises in Otsego Lake.

SUSQUEHANNA RIVER

Its Algonquin name means "the river of the long reaches." The Susquehanna begins in Cooperstown and extends down to Baltimore and the Chesapeake Bay.

At the time that the Erie Canal was opened, it was hoped that "Clinton's Ditch" would soon be connected to the head of Otsego Lake, and the northern stretch of the river would be made navigable by means of locks and canals. Such a plan would have created continuous water transportation from the Great Lakes through the center of New York, Pennsylvania, and Maryland to the Atlantic Ocean.

OTSEGO LAKE,
COOPERSTOWN, N.Y.

216738

CLINTON DAM MARKER

In 1779, General Clinton's troops erected a log dam to raise the level of the lake. When the dam was broken, the depth of the river increased appreciatively for a distance of a hundred miles. This provided the Continental Army with enough water to navigate the river with their bateaux and thus unite with General Sullivan's army near Binghamton.

Traces of the dam were still visible in 1839, but most of the logs had been ceremoniously removed in 1825 as the village celebrated the opening of the Erie Canal and looked forward to the building of the never realized "Susquehanna River Canal."

KINGFISHER TOWER, OTSEGO LAKE, COOPERSTOWN, N. Y.

KINGFISHER TOWER

Back in 1876 when the fantastically rich Edward Clark wanted a private picnic area, he purchased Point Judith about two miles up the east side of the lake and erected a Swiss chalet type of cottage. But this touch of Europe was apparently too light for the cultured Mr. Clark, so he conceived that what the lake really needed was a medieval castle. The consequence of this thought was a minature castle of some sixty feet in height and twenty feet square at the base. Constructed of stone taken from the shores of the lake, the tower has ramparts and parapets (as every good castle should) and platforms in the tower from which to view the lake.

Docks showing steamers — Otsego Lake.

FAIR STREET DOCKS

Boats have toured the lake for many years. In 1794, an excentric man called Admiral Hassy launched a wooden boat to fish from and thus make his living. The boat used boards for sails. This was followed, thirty years later, by a cabined craft that used horses on treadmills to turn a paddlewheel. It wasn't a great success.

The first reliable steamboat to tour the lake was a retired Civil War gunboat that was transported to Cooperstown in 1870. Shortly after came the larger vessels such as the prominent one pictured here, the Mohican.

Steamer Mohican.   Otsego Lake, N. Y.

STEAMER MOHICAN

The Mohican was the last of the large (400 passenger capacity) tourist boats to ply the waters of the lake. It was launched in 1905 and conducted regular service until 1931. August A. Busch, the wealthy brewer, bought the boat then and moved it to his Three-Mile Point estate where it was dismantled in 1935.

Coincidentally, the Chief Uncas, the beautiful wooden boat which a few years ago resumed the tourist trips, was bought from the Busch estate.

8434. Muskrat Castle, on Sunken Island, Otsego Lake, N. Y.

MUSKRAT CASTLE

The "Muskrat Castle" postcard is an artist's rendering of the habitation of the fictional character, Tom Hutter, of Cooper's "The Deerslayer." It was supposedly located in the northern section of the lake on a shoal known as Sunken Island.

Although "Muskrat Castle" may never have existed except on the pages of a book, the "Ark," the cabined raft featured in that same novel was "reconstructed" by a motion picture company which produced the first "Deerslayer" movie on the lake in 1911.

Three—Mile Point, Otsego Lake

THREE MILE POINT, COOPERSTOWN

Since the very early days of Cooperstown, Three Mile Point has been a favorite recreation spot for the villagers. So it was in 1837 when it was owned by James Fenimore Cooper. But in that year, in reaction to an incident of vandalism done to the property, the author forbade its use by anyone who did not have his special permission. The citizens of Cooperstown were incensed by this as well as Cooper's apparent snobbery, and at a mass meeting they proposed that the edict be disregarded and his books banned from the village library. Newspapers throughout the state took up the controversy, and the novelist sued them for libel.

Five Mile Point Inn,
Otsego Lake, N. Y.

FIVE MILE POINT INN

Five Mile Point has been the location of a resort since 1851. The original building burned
in 1908 and was replaced the next year by the
structure pictured here. But the company that
erected the new inn could not keep in business,
and in 1918, the building was turned into a private residence.

In 1928 when the wealthy August A. Busch
offered to swap with the village, the point and
the inn for Three-Mile Point (which was between
his estate and the lake), the villagers, remem-
bering how hard they fought through the years
to gain and keep their treasured recreation spot,
declined the offer.

24

Otsego Lake Park, Cooperstown, N. Y.

OTSEGO LAKE PARK

Otsego Lake Park was located at the foot of Pioneer Street and was run as a private concern that catered to the new flow of tourists that the electric trolley brought. Besides being a good spot to view the lake and socialize, row boats and motor boats were rented there.

The pavilion was erected in 1902. That same year, the Otsego Lake Tally-ho Company which provided transportation between Cooperstown and Richfield Springs, via boat and stagecoach, was put out of business by the trolley.

The park property was later given to the village, and the pavilion was removed in the 1930's.

Main Street. Cooperstown, N. Y.

MAIN STREET AND TROLLEY

The electric trolley ran from Oneonta to Rich-field Springs via Hartwick and Schuyler Lake. It reached Cooperstown by way of a branch line at Index. The line forked at Chestnut St. to run up Grove to Main. The other line went up chestnut as far as Main and then over to Pioneer. In 1917, the Main St. section was torn up with the line ending then at the depot on the north side of the street. There was also a freight station at Beaver St.

Passenger service on the trolley was discontinued in 1933, and on September 16, 1940, the last freight train, a carload of coal for the Beach Coal Company, made its run.

STREET DECORATIONS, CENTENNIAL CELEBRATION, AUG. 4 -10th, 1907, COOPERSTOWN, N.Y.

CENTENNIAL CELEBRATION

1886, not 1907, was the year that the Coopers-town Centennial should have been celebrated, but the good citizens of that former year did not think to raise a celebration. By 1907, how-ever, they were more in the mood, so a disused act of village incorporation passed in 1807 was used as an excuse to throw a party.

Worse than the fact that the celebration was for an act that was never put into effect was that this same act called the village "Otsego" to replace the name "Cooperstown" which it had always had. Nevertheless, in one day the celebration drew an unprecedented 15,000 people to the village.

Main Street, Cooperstown, N. Y.

MAIN STREET

The great fire of 1862 leveled nearly all of the buildings on Main Street from about where this picture was taken to as far east as Pioneer Street. The only structure that escaped destruction was the stone Cory Building, later known as the Stone Jug (first fully pictured building on the left). Built in 1829 as a hardware store, it was, at that time, the spot where many of the townspeople gathered. James Fenimore Cooper and Chief Justice Samuel Nelson met there frequently to discuss the problems of the day.

The Cory Building was torn down in 1930 to make room for a chain store.

CORNER OF CHESTNUT AND MAIN STREET, SHOWING VILLAGE HALL, COOPERSTOWN, N. Y.

VILLAGE HALL, COOPERSTOWN

Constructed in 1889, the ground floor of the brick building housed the fire department and the headquarters of the village trustees. A large auditoriun with a gallery that could accommodate five hundred people was located on the second floor. It had a stage with a curtain with a design that depicted a scene from "The Pioneers."

In 1916, William C. Smalley leased the hall and began the community's first movie theatre.

The bell tower was removed from the building in 1949 when it was judged unsafe. The building itself was demolished to make way for the new village structure now on the site.

New D. & H. passenger depot at Cooperstown, N. Y.

NEW D&H PASSENGER DEPOT

One of the conditions agreed to by the Delaware & Hudson when it bought the Cooperstown & Susquehanna Valley Railroad was that they would build a new station "... of such architecture, size, and general character in keeping with the dignity, importance and historic character of the village."

Built in 1916, the station has the herringbone style stonework of the first stone house in the village (still standing on the corner of Main and River Streets). It served as a station for less than twenty years and is now a private home.

Cooperstown, N.Y. Otsego Hall, Cooper's Home. Built 1798, Burned 1852.

OTSEGO HALL

William Cooper was a New Jersey Quaker who bought unseen a sizeable chunk of wilderness and came up to what is now the village that bears his name to see it settled and his fortune made. When these goals were accomplished, he built a noble house in the very center of the group of streets he had plotted out.

Otsego Hall stood in the middle of what is now the Cooper Grounds. The picture shows the building with the Gothic alterations that were added by James Fenimore Cooper with the assistance of Samuel Morse.

The year after the novelist died, the mansion was destroyed by a fire of suspicious origin.

The Cooper Grounds,
Site of the Home of James Fenimore Cooper
COOPERSTOWN, N. Y. The Fotograf Co.

Cooperstown, N.Y. Christ Church.

CHRIST CHURCH

The first rector of Christ Church was Rev. Daniel Nash. Father Nash seems to have been the quintessential pioneer minister. Arriving at the town of Exeter in 1797, Father Nash administered to the religious needs of a far-flung flock. His missionary journeys took him to nine counties in central New York, and he reached them on horseback with his wife riding behind him and each of them holding one of their children in their arms.

James Fenimore Cooper apparently used him as the model for Rev. Mr. Grant, a character in "The Pioneers." And Cooper also altered his simple church into a gothic structure.

J. FENIMORE COOPER'S GRAVE, COOPERSTOWN, N.Y.

JAMES FENIMORE COOPER'S GRAVE

James Fenimore Cooper died in Cooperstown on September 14, 1851, the day before his sixty-second birthday. His body was on view at Otsego Hall just a few feet from Christ Churchyard where he is buried.

The novelist, known through his youth as plain "James Cooper," once attempted to change his name to James Cooper Fenimore in order to satisfy his mother who was distressed that there were no men left to carry out her family name. The court, however, would not allow the change, so he adopted "Fenimore" as his middle name.

Cooperstown, N. Y. Clark Estate & Entrance to Cooper Park.

CLARK ESTATE OFFICES, COOPERSTOWN

Edward Clark was practicing law in New York City in 1848 when a tinkering genius named Isaac M. Singer came into his office with legal problems concerning rights to a machine he had invented. Clark sorted them out successfully and realized that what Mr. Singer needed was legal organization. They formed an equal partnership, and when Mr. Singer's sewing machine was put on the market, both men made a fortune. Mr. Clark, who had married a local woman, put some of his money in Cooperstown real estate.

In 1897, Clark Estates took over the old Otsego County Bank Building (built 1831).

Cooperstown, N.Y.   Y.M.C.A. and Library.

Y.M.C.A. AND LIBRARY

The Clarks were responsible in 1898 for the construction of the large stone building on the corner of Main and Fair Streets. It was form-ally opened with a ball given by Mrs. Alfred Corning Clark in honor of the twenty-first birthday of her son.

The building was first used as a YMCA. Their library was the predecessor of what is now the Village Library. Changed to the Village Club in 1911, the building also functioned as the first home of the Baseball Hall of Fame (1935), and it was also the first Cooperstown home of the New York State Historical Association when it moved here from Ticonderoga in 1938.

"Fernleigh," Residence of Mrs. Henry C. Potter
COOPERSTOWN, N. Y.

FERNLEIGH

Originally known as "Apple Hill" until renamed
by Edward Clark when he built his new mansion
there in 1869, the Fernleigh property (east side
of River Street) has been the home of many note-
worthy persons. Richard Cooper, the oldest
brother of James, built a house there in 1800.

Later, Chief Justice of the U.S. Supreme Court
Samuel Nelson resided there. Another tenant
was John A. Dix, Secretary of the Treasury at
the outbreak of the Civil War, U. S. Senator,
and Governor of New York. A military school
   The Henry C. Potter mentioned in the card
was the Episcopal Bishop of New York. He married the widow of Alfred Corning Clark.

Otsego Hall, Cooperstown, N. Y.

OTSEGO HALL BOARDING HOUSE

The village of Cooperstown is called "Temple-ton" in "The Pioneers," and its founder, made in the image of William Cooper, is "Judge Temple." The grand house in which he lives is "Templeton Lodge," and it resembles the Otsego Hall which burned in 1852.

When a large boarding house for summer guests was constructed on Nelson Avenue near the lake in 1885, the owners dubbed it Temple-ton Lodge. Twelve years later, however, the name was curiously changed to Otsego Hall, as if to give up the pretense of the fictional title.

Otsego Hall was a popular resort until torn down by the Clark Estates in 1930.

HOTEL FENIMORE

HOTEL FENIMORE

The Hotel Fenimore, which stood on the north-east corner of Main and Chestnut, was built by Edward Clark in 1874 and operated as a summer hotel through most of its existence. It was the place where the wealthy stayed (John D. Rockefeller in 1922).

Apparently, the establishment was never very successful despite numerous injections of money for periodic renovations. The old hotel had many owners and experienced a number of closings which were due to financial difficulty. The building was finally razed in 1935 to improve the grounds when the Willowbrook Mansion was made into the Cooper Inn.

COOPER INN

It was not until 1936 that the brick mansion on Chestnut Street became the Cooper Inn. It had previously been a private residence called "Willowbrook." It was built in 1816 by Henry Phinney who, with his brother, ran the publishing company which had brought the first newspaper to Otsego County. But the company's main enterprise was the publishing of books. This they carried out in their building on Pioneer Street. They also had many bookstores in towns as far away as Buffalo and Detroit and traveling bookstores on wagons and canal boats.

The publishing company moved from Cooperstown after arsonists burned their building.

40

Hotel Ote-sa-ga. COOPERSTOWN, N. Y.

HOTEL OTE-SA-GA, COOPERSTOWN

The first attempt at establishing a large resort hotel in Cooperstown was back in 1869 when building commenced on a large brick structure on the corner of Main and Fair Streets. Unfortunately, the $57,000 spent on the building (a sizeable sum back in those days) was not enough, and the building stood, an unfinished eyesore dubbed the "Skeleton Hotel," until removed in 1889. The only use to which it was ever put was as a place to store hops.

The village has had a number of small hotels and even the larger Fenimore Hotel, but it wasn't until Edward Severin Clark built the Otesaga that the village received its fine, large resort.

60011

OTESAGA HOTEL-KNOX SCHOOL

Built in 1909, the Otesaga suffered during the depression of the 1930's when it was forced to close as a summer hotel until after the war.

But during that time it still continued its winter function as the Knox School for Girls. The school moved to Long Island in 1954.

During the 1960's, the A. T. & T. Corporation used it as a training center.

Hoffman House. Cooperstown, N. Y.

HOFFMAN HOUSE

Demolished in 1932, the Hoffman House stood at the corner of Main Street and Hoffman Lane. The large structure was actually two buildings, a residence and a store, connected in 1876 to form a hotel. It was first known as the Globe, and later as the Ballard House, the Park Hotel, and, finally, the Hoffman House.

The post office now occupies the spot pictured.

Thanksgiving Hospital, Cooperstown, N. Y.

THANKSGIVING HOSPITAL, COOPERSTOWN

Hospital care in Cooperstown started with the Thanksgiving Hospital on Grove Street. Founded in gratitude for the end of the Civil War and through the efforts of Susan Cooper, the institution was opened in 1868 and enlarged over the years.

After the larger Bassett Hospital was opened, Thanksgiving Hospital was converted to use as a home for older people.

MARY IMOGENE BASSETT HOSPITAL

MARY IMOGENE BASSETT HOSPITAL

In 1917, Edward Severin Clark and Mary Imogene Bassett (the daughter of two Otsego County physicians as well as a physician herself) felt the need for a more modern facility than Thanksgiving Hospital. They began the work on a new building of fieldstone gotten from the demolition of the old Utica Knitting Company plant at Phoenix Mills. But with the First World War continuing, the nearly completed hospital as well as other Clark buildings in the village were loaned to the Army Air Corps for use as an officers' convalescent center. Five hundred aviators were treated there from 1917 to 1919.

The hospital opened to the public in the 1920's.

COURT HOUSE, COOPERSTOWN, N. Y.

COURTHOUSE

A log and frame structure at the southeast corner of Main and Pioneer Streets was the first Otsego County Courthouse. The traditional stocks stood in front. This building was used for sixteen years until a new brick building was erected in 1807 near the present courthouse. This burned in 1840 and was replaced by another structure that was condemned in 1879.

The towered, red brick structure still in use was designed by Archimedes Russell who did many prominent buildings around the state.

Court House and
County Clerks Office,
Cooperstown, N. Y.

COUNTY CLERK'S OFFICE

Although Cooperstown has always been the county seat, there was once a move on for the lower half of the county to "secede" from Otsego. In 1866, the town of Oneonta attempted to form a new county composed of the towns along the southern tier. This new county was to be called "Susquehanna," and, of course, its seat was to be the village of Oneonta.

Another endeavor tried to move the seat of government for the whole county to Oneonta when a new courthouse was needed in 1879. But Cooperstown managed to raise $10,000 to help pay for a new building.

The clerk's office stood from 1901 until 1970.

City of Oneonta

GREETINGS FROM ONEONTA, N. Y.

STATE ARMORY

U. & D. DEPOT

D. & H. DEPOT

D. & H. ROUND HOUSE

Birds-eye view of Oneonta, N. Y., from Armory Tower

BIRDSEYE VIEW, ONEONTA

The hamlet was called McDonald's Mills when it started life around the beginning of the nineteenth century. When the first postoffice was opened in 1817, it became known as Milfordville, it then being a part of the township of Milford. When the new township was formed in 1830, they called it Oneonta, the old Indian word meaning "the place of open rocks."

MAIN STREET. ONEONTA. N. Y.

MAIN STREET

Like a number of thoroughfares in central New York, Oneonta's Main Street began as an Indian trail— a path twelve to fifteen inches wide and worn to a depth of a foot in some places. The Main Street trail skirted the edge of the hill which led to the marsh lands which bordered the nearby Susquehanna. So close to the street was the river, that when high its waters lapped the slope near the trail.

A flood over a century ago changed the course of the river to its present more southern position. But by then, the location of the village was fixed along the old river trail.

Main Street North from the New Hotel, Oneonta, N.Y.

12446

MAIN STREET LOOKING NORTH

During Oneonta's early years, it seemed that the center of the village would be down at River Street where a tavern as well as the only mill were located. But the center changed when the Charlotte Turnpike was organized. It ran from Harpersfield through West Davenport, crossing the river at Emmons and then down Main to Chestnut and then up that street to reach West Oneonta.

The road was heavily traveled, and taverns erected at the corner of Chestnut and Main were patronized by passing drovers.

Main St. Cor. Chestnut St., as it was in 1860, Site of the Baird Block, Oneonta, N. Y.

MAIN STREET AT CHESTNUT, 1860

The view here is looking west from the south side of Main Street. Chestnut Street is between the two large buildings. The larger building is the Susquehanna House; the other, the Oneonta House. The area in front of the two inns was the scene of many political rallies and various celebrations. Among the most festive of gatherings was the one of August 29, 1865. On this day flags and bunting decorated the balconies, and dozens of flowered archs spanned the streets. Bands played, cannons boomed, and handkerchiefs waved as the whole town cheered the arrival of the first train from Albany and the beginning of the village's prosperity.

D. & H. Station, Oneonta, N.Y.

D & H DEPOT

The builders of the Romanesque style depot (1892) at the foot of Broad Street were apparently well aware that the structure was to be the city's front door. The high turrets have greeted many train passengers, and the arched doorways have welcomed them. In the best of times, lady travelers were presented flowers from the railroad's greenhouse.

Everyday, a half dozen trains in each direction on the Albany—Binghamton line stopped here. The last passenger train of the D&H left Oneonta on January 24, 1963.

D & H ROUNDHOUSE

The first roundhouse in Oneonta was built in 1870 on land that was formerly a swamp. Made of Oneonta stone and brick and cement from Howe's Cave, the structure was added to many times over the years. The roundhouse pictured was erected in 1906 and was the largest in the world.

The railroad has done much for Oneonta since its arrival in 1865 and the building of the first shops in the 1870's. Indeed, the population of the village quadrupled from 744 in 1865 to 3,004 in 1880 and leaped to 4,518 four years later. Many worked in the shops where the cars were made and the huge engines repaired.

The D. & H. Tracks at Oneonta, N. Y.

Main St. Cor. Dietz, as it was in 1874, Oneonta, N. Y.

MAIN ST. CORNER AT DIETZ, 1874

The Bissell Block, on the corner, was built in 1866 and has managed to escape fires and urban renewal. The section with the awning next to the hardware store around this time housed a music hall. The trees and fence next to the building surrounded two private homes whose grounds extended back to near the present Huntington Park.

Note the columned Susquehanna House up the block with a barely discernible structure between it and the trees. This is the present Novelty Lounge (1838) before its stamped, sheet iron facade of 1892 replaced the original stone front. The tall building is the Stanton Opera Hse.

Main St., Covered Bridge over Susquehanna River, Oneonta, N. Y., as it was in 1885

MAIN STREET, COVERED BRIDGE

When the Franklin Turnpike was built, a good bridge to span the river was needed. In 1835, a wooden covered bridge was erected near the present site of the Main Street bridge.

It was constructed of clear, hand-hewn pine, the timbers being joined with large oak pins. This covered bridge lasted until 1888 when it was replaced by one of iron.

Main Stree. River Bridge, Oneonta, N. Y.

MAIN STREET RIVER BRIDGE

Constructed in 1889, this was the fourth river bridge at Main Street. It replaced the covered bridge and, made of iron, was regarded as one of the wonders of the area. At the time of its opening, the Oneonta Weekly Spy editorialized, "... we hope it may endure until at least 1999, or a century or two longer. Long before that time street cars will cross on that bridge or another, and the South Side wards will be counted by thousands of people."

The iron structure was condemned in 1930. The present bridge is the second one built since then.

HORSE-DRAWN RAILWAY

The Oneonta Street Railway was started in the summer of 1888 as a horse-drawn railway. The Wilber family put up most of the $20,000 needed to start the road which began service with two and a quarter miles of track extending from the East End village line down Main Street to Chestnut and then up as far as Fonda. The company's equipment was kept in barns at Reynolds Street. The fare for the run was five cents.

Cars were also chartered for special uses, a frequent run being that to convey funeral parties to the cemeteries in the village.

Main Street looking East—North Side, Oneonta, N.Y.

ELECTRIC TROLLEY ON MAIN STREET

Electric trolley service in Oneonta got off to a bad start when the trial run in August of 1898 knocked out most of the telephone service. Operation of the line was stopped by court order. But the problem was soon rectified, and the trolley days blossomed.

Railways were extended in the city and soon out to West Oneonta. In 1901, Cooperstown was reached via Laurens, Mount Vision, Hartwick, and a junction at Index. A route to Richfield Springs was constructed the year after.

60

Maple St.
Oneonta N.Y.

MAPLE STREET AND TROLLEY

Until 1923, there was an extension of the trolley line that led up Maple Street to the Normal School. Neighborhood boys would give the operators on this branch a difficult time. They would hitch rides on the trolley bumpers and pull free the pole that connected the trolley to its power line. Coating the rails on the Maple Street hill with slippery, wet leaves was another of their amusements.

It was probably the prevalence of such antics as these that prompted the 1885 ordinance forbidding snowballing on many of the village streets.

High School, Oneonta, N. Y.

ONEONTA HIGH SCHOOLS

Oneonta's first school was a log cabin built where Broad Street once joined Main. Split logs mounted on crude legs of the appropriate lengths were used for the desks and the seats. A frame structure replaced this building at the same location in 1812.

The Union School pictured above was built on Academy Street in 1868 and enlarged later to three times its original size. This wooden school was replaced in 1907 by the yellow brick and limestone structure which was later used as part of the Junior High complex.

ONEONTA HIGH SCHOOL, ONEONTA, N. Y.

State Normal School, Oneonta, N. Y.

OLD MAIN

The huge "Old Main" building (160 rooms) which was razed in 1977 was actually not the original building of Oneonta State Normal School but an almost duplicate replacement of a structure which burned down in 1894, a mere five years after it was completed.

The first head of the school was Dr. James M. Milne, a dedicated educator committed to the advancement of the most progressive teaching methods of his time. A scandal broke out in 1897 concerning Dr. Milne and a young lady teacher. The student body overwhelmingly backed their principal, but George I. Wilber and other members of the school board ousted him.

STATE NORMAL SCHOOL

Needless to say, school rules in the early days of the Normal were very strict. Of course, if you were a student, you couldn't smoke on school property, and drinking was forbidden. In fact, if you were caught simply being in an establish- ment where liquor was sold, you were expelled. You could go out on dates, but if you happened to be female, your date (both the man and the place to which you were going) first had to be approved by the Dean of Women. You would also need special permission to ride in an automo- bile no matter what sex you were.

Broad Street, Oneonta, N. Y.

BROAD STREET

Totally devastated by the urban renewal plan of the early 1970's, Broad Street is now a sad and empty space. But for over a century it had been an area of activity in the city's very center.

The street was created in 1863 in preparation for the building of the first railroad depot and the coming of the Albany and Susquehanna in 1865. With the station at the foot of old Broad and the large hotel block at its head, the street functioned as a place of great commerce. A large cigar factory had once been located here as well as a farming machinery maker, a distillery, a livery stable, a hotel, a movie theatre, and The Daily Star plant.

Oneonta Milling Co.'s Buildings and Water Power Supply, Oneonta, N. Y.

ONEONTA MILLING COMPANY

Until the 1960's, there had been a grist mill on the site of the old Elmore mill near the foot of the Main Street viaduct since the first settling of the area in the 1780's. Settlers came from miles around to grind their grain there and barter a portion of their crop for supplies.

Because of the mill, then, the first stores were built and the first tavern opened, and a village began.

The Elmore Company bought the plant in 1896. And in 1918 a German sabotage attempt was suspected when a loaded shotgun shell was found in the highly combustible flour dust on top of the grinding plates, and a spy was arrested.

State Armory, Oneonta, N. Y.

STATE ARMORY

When news that the Great War was finally over reached Oneonta on November 11, 1918, the town down went wild in impromptu celebration. The Star received the news at 3:45 AM, and the presses were stopped and a new front page set. The fire department and the D&H were then no- tified, and all the whistles, bells, and sirens in town sounded to awake the citizens to the news.

A huge bonfire was started at Broad and Main Streets. The mayor declared a holiday, and there was a parade and a huge meeting at the Armory. Here there was music, and town leaders gave speeches that said that there would never again be another war.

POST OFFICE. ONEONTA, N. Y.

POST OFFICE

Oneonta's first post office was at the McDonald Tavern at the corner of Main and River Streets. It has had sixteen different locations, mostly on Main but also on Dietz. When the office was in the Central Hotel building, the postmaster, Harlow Bundy, tested there an employee time recorder invented by his brother, Willard. The results were successful, and production of the recorders was started in Binghamton. The Bundy invention was the start of IBM.

The pillared structure on Main Street was opened in 1915 and used as a post office until 1967.

Post-Office, Oneonta, N. Y.

DIETZ STREET

When the Dietz brothers opened a thoroughfare through their farm land in 1853, they created one of the village's busiest streets.

In order to insure that the street would touch on a maximum amount of Dietz land, they had to create a bend near the present Wall Street.

Here one of the brothers built his home (presently the site of a parking lot). The other Dietz built his residence where the street ended at what is now Walnut Street.

The country origins of the town can be discerned in the first name that the street had, namely, Shanghai Street, after a breed of chickens that were numerous there.

63. HUNTINGTON PARK AND PUBLIC LIBRARY, ONEONTA, N. Y.

HUNTINGTON PARK AND LIBRARY

Huntington Library was the former home of Solon Huntington (brother of Collis, the California railroad builder) and was given to the village by his son, Henry, a noted art collector and heir to his uncle's huge fortune. It was Henry who also founded the other Huntington Library in Los Angeles.

The park behind the library was also a part of the gift. A part of the park fronting on Dietz St. had been the location of the Metropolitan Theatre where early vaudeville performers such as the Cohan family played.

The rotunda pictured in the card was demolished in 1965.

Hotel Windsor, Oneonta, N.Y.

216512

HOTEL WINDSOR

The Windsor was built (1884) on the south corner of Chestnut and Wall Streets on the site of one of the city's first industries, Seeber's tannery (c. 1812-1830). Traces of the old tanks and vats were found while excavating for the foundations of the hotel.

In its day, the Hotel Windsor was one of the most important buildings in the city. It had 108 rooms and the only passenger elevator in town. When Main Street received its first section of pavement (using blocks of chestnut wood), the hard surface way was extended up Chestnut St. as far as the hotel.

23 - Central Hotel, Oneonta, N. Y.

CENTRAL HOTEL

Constructed in 1873 by Alfred C. Lewis, the Central Hotel at one time housed the First National Bank, Herrieff's Clothes Shop, the National Express Company, and Ingerham's Barbershop. An 1887 publication had this description of the town's largest hotel: "The Central has eighty rooms, each with its separate steam heat radiator and electric bell; the house is lighted throughout with gas, and there are bath rooms on every floor." It also had a fine dining room that was for many years the city's social center.

Stages left daily from the building's Main St. entrance for Morris, Laurens, and Delhi.

Ruins, Central Hotel Fire, Oneonta, N. Y., Jan. 16th 1910

CENTRAL HOTEL FIRE

The fire that destroyed the Central Hotel was discovered in the boiler room at 3:15 AM, Jan. 16, 1910. It spread quickly through the original brick veneer section and then through open fire doors to the solid brick section at the Dietz St. corner (the section left standing in the picture).

Temperatures reading below zero hindered the fighting of the fire, and the Lewis Building to the east was also damaged. Although there were three deaths, most of the occupants of the hotel managed to escape via regular exits, through windows and down ropes and ladders and through a covered bridge which connected the second floor with the Lewis Building.

ONEONTA HOTEL, ONEONTA, N. Y.

HOTEL ONEONTA

Built in 1911 on the site of the old Central Hotel, the Hotel Oneonta at one time had a billiard parlor and bowling alleys in its basement, and the City Club, complete with ballroom, was housed on its top floor. Radio station WDOS made its first broadcasts from studios there.

One of the persons responsible for building the Oneonta was Herbert T. Jennings, the man who had successfully extended the Oneonta & Otego Valley Railroad to Richfield Springs and Mohawk. When the hotel was finished, the entrepreneur went into banking. Within three months, his two banks failed; he went to prison.

Published by Oneonta Department Store   **Ruins of Oneonta's $75,000 Fire, May 22, 1906.**

FIRE, MAY 22, 1906

Downtown suffered many fires around the turn of the century. Businesses on Main Street and Broad Street were the most often hit.

Begun in the early morning of May 22, 1906, this famous conflagration was known as the Wil-ber Block Fire. It destroyed the four story Wilber National Bank, which stood where the head of South Main Street is now, and the two buildings next to it. The fire threatened the entire south side of the street, and an appeal to Cooperstown for help brought a special train with 150 men and fire-fighting apparatus.

Municipal Building, Oneonta, N. Y.

MUNICIPAL BUILDING

The Main Street fire of 1906 caused the citizens of Oneonta to feel uneasy about their old wooden Municipal Building which had narrowly escaped the flames. The following year, they thought it best to take down the old structure before it burned down. They then built this brick struc-ture which served its purpose until 1981.

The other building in the picture is the Wescott Block (1886) which was razed in 1968. Among its many tenants was the Casino, Oneonta's first movie theatre.

A replica of the town clock on the top of the Wescott was placed on the Municipal building in 1977. It includes parts from the original.

ELECTRIC LIGHT PLANT AND FALLS, ONEONTA, N. Y.

ELECTRIC LIGHT PLANT AND FALLS

In the early days of electricity, power was available only from dusk to dawn, and rates were on a per-lamp basis rather than by the present kilowatt hour system.

This hydroplant, fed Susquehanna water from a bulkhead on that river, was located at East End and was built in 1897 to replace a power plant (steam engines) which was on Gas Ave.

Electric Lake was a pond of some fifty acres, and aside from its intended purpose, it also provided ice for cutting in winter and a place for fishing and swimming in summer.

The water wheel and control gates were removed after operation ceased in 1954.

A "Big" Day at the Oneonta Fair, Oneonta, N. Y.

CENTRAL NEW YORK FAIR

The first Oneonta Fair was in 1874, and for fifty-two years it was the city's biggest annual event. Schools were let off for two afternoons, and downtown stores stayed open late into the evening for the occasion.

Taking place a week after Syracuse's State Fair, the Oneonta gathering received many of the acts and exhibits directly from there. In 1910, 30,000 people attended the fair in a single day arriving by special excursion trains from as far away as Scranton, Albany, and Kingston.

Horse racing was held on a circular course that is now Belmont Circle, and this and the area surrounding was the fair grounds.

THE PONY FARM, ONEONTA N. Y.   553   MILLARD & KEENAN

THE PONY FARM

The raising and selling of Shetland ponies started out as a hobby for Malcolm G. Keenan in the early years of this century. But the hobby became a business, and the business took the form of a partnership with L. C. Millard (who also ran the Central Hotel). Soon the "farm" had to be moved from the barn behind Keenan's home at 10 Walnut Street to property on the Plains west of the city.

Their herd of about fifty ponies traveled under their own power to fairs in Otsego and neighboring counties where rides were given to thrill children and tempt parents to buy the pets.

The Pony Farm was sold in 1918.

Corner Walnut and Dietz Streets,
Oneonta, N. Y.

THE MOORE HOUSE

The Queen Anne style of architecture was a favorite at the turn of the century, and evidence of this is found throughout the county. An example is the house on the corner of Dietz and Walnut Streets built in 1895 by George Moore, a local druggist and father of the late Edwin R. Moore. Ed Moore was the Star reporter whose local history column, "Oneonta, Past and Present," was a regular feature of that newspaper. The now out-of-print collections of these columns are treasured by everyone interested in the history of the greater Oneonta area.

ONEONTA DEPARTMENT STORE

In the nineteenth century, Yankee peddlers traveled the countryside in large wagons jangling with pots and pans, tools and toys, cloves and cloth, and countless other items. Some of these salesmen, of course, were the dishonest sort that sold quantities of wooden nutmeg and then moved on. Others were fair businesspersons who circled the areas of their homes on regular routes. Frank H. Bresee was of this latter kind, and he soon saw that a string of permanent stores would be better than a traveling one.

At the age of twenty, he opened his first store in South Hartwick and soon after other small stores. In 1899, he opened the Oneonta branch.

216503

FOX MEMORIAL HOSPITAL AND NURSES' HOME, ONEONTA, N. Y.

FOX MEMORIAL HOSPITAL

Fox Memorial Hospital was started when a local businessman, ex-army officer (Civil War), and prominent politician donated $10,000 in memory of his wife. He later willed most of his estate to the hospital with the only stipulation being that it would always be called the Aurelia Osborn Fox Memorial Hospital.

Fox was chartered in 1900. Prior to this, however, there was a private hospital run by Rachael Bliss on High Street. This was incorporated into the Oneonta Hospital Society in 1895.

84

A Main Street Residence, Oneonta, N. Y.

FAIRCHILD MANSION

The Masonic Temple on the corner of Main and Grand had until 1929 been a private home. The oldest portion of the brick house was built in 1867 by David J. Yager, but the present appearance of the building dates from the turn of the century when extensive remodeling was done by the wealthy George W. Fairchild, organizer of IBM. He added the tower, the third floor, and the red tile roof.

Inside, the building was given the improvements of six fireplaces, a mahogany library, a dining room with mahogany beams and panelling and French tapestry, and a similar cardroon

The Masons bought the property in 1929.

ONEONTA CLUB

Having the seed of its birth in the city's volunteer fire company, the Oneonta Club was headquartered at the Dietz Street building erected for that purpose in 1886. Like similar organizations of its day, it was a place where men gathered (Women were not permitted except at the monthly dances.).

Richly furnished, the building housed lounges, a large billiard room, bowling alleys in the basement, and card rooms and a ballroom on the second floor. Here, in overstuffed chairs before mantled fireplaces, the men of power sat planning matters of business and politics.

The building is now the Lewis Funeral Home.

Chestnut Street and Methodist Church,
Oneonta, N. Y.

CHESTNUT ST. AND METHODIST CHURCH

This structure, on the sight of the present church, was built in 1869. In 1886, it was enlarged and veneered in brick and thus used until razed in 1925.

Visible above the trolley is the brick home of George B. Baird which later became the Physicians Building in 1939 and then torn down when the supermarket was built. This same corner lot was once the site of the Collis P. Huntington homestead, and in 1879 was planned to be the site for the new county courthouse when Oneonta battled Cooperstown to be the seat of government.

Towns

Mayne's Store, Burlington Flats, N. Y.

MAYNE'S STORE, BURLINGTON FLATS

The country store grew out of the traveling peddler tradition. Indeed, many of the first storekeepers were itinerant peddlers who decided to settle down.

The old stores were all stores rolled into one. They sold medicine and shoes, plows and buttons and tea and tobacco. In the early days of the settlers, when government issued money was scarce, jugs of whiskey were used as currency. The farmer traded his grain to the distiller for whiskey, and the whiskey was traded at the country store for clothing or tools or other needed supplies.

The store pictured still stands unchanged.

BURLINGTON FLATS SCHOOL

In the early days of the country, a farmer and millwright from Burlington, Jedidiah Peck, battled the wealthy Federalist William Cooper on the issue of voting rights. The Federalists believed that only wealthy landowners should have the vote, and for a while they seemed to have their way. But when Cooper had his opponent arrested under the Alien and Sedition Act (which made speaking out against the government a crime), he made the ordinary farmer a martyr for the Jeffersonian cause.

In the end, the Jeffersonians won; the Sedition Act was repealed, and Peck went on to fight for the common man's right to an education.

Baptist Church
Burlington, N.Y.

BAPTIST CHURCH, BURLINGTON GREEN

Burlington Green or "Yankeetown" was a stopping point on the Great Western Turnpike that led from Albany and Cherry Valley to Sherburne. It was also the point where this road was crossed by the old Indian trail connecting the early settlements of the Garretts and the Tunnicliffes (Exeter).

Quite naturally, hotels and stores sprung up at the crossroads, and the little village nestled between two of the steepest grades along the turnpike became a noted spot among travelers.

The town is named for Burlington, New Jersey where early owners of the property were from.

78—View from the Stone Quarry, Gilbertsville, N. Y.

GILBERTSVILLE, TOWN OF BUTTERNUTS

The town of Butternuts received its name from a growth of butternut which formed three trees from a single trunk and marked a boundary for the first land patents.

The village of Gilbertsville began with the arrival of the Englishman Abijah Gilbert to the area in 1787. Mr. Gilbert came by way of New Jersey where, sight unseen, he purchased one thousand acres of Butternut Valley land from the Morrises.

The residents of this beautiful valley village have since 1936 successfully fought off the attempts of the Army Corps of Engineers to construct a dam that would turn the area into a lake.

43—Gilbertsville, High School, Gilbertsville, N. Y.

GILBERTSVILLE HIGH SCHOOL

During the nineteenth century, Gilbertsville Academy and Collegiate Institute was a well known institution. Built in 1839 and enlarged at another time, the building was later taken over by the public school system and used for a number of years as a high school. The stone structure is still standing.

Looking down Commercial St., Gilbertsville, N.Y.

MAJOR'S INN, GILBERTSVILLE

In 1895, a fire destroyed the large Stag's Head Inn which stood on the present site of the park know as The Overlook (shown being constructed) and the 1821 Gilbert Homestead. In 1897, the Major's Inn was constructed on the site of the homestead using some of its stonework. The inn was built by Major J. L. Gilbert and served as the family home until the major's death in 1904. It then became a public inn. A large dining room was added in 1917.

The building was sold at a tax sale in 1975 for a very small sum but still stands among the many other gracious Gilbertsville mansions that were erected in the resort era.

Historic Cherry Valley, N. Y.
Old Toll Gate

Soldiers Barracks 1862

Soldiers Monument

Monument Commemorating the Massacre of 1778

National Central Bank

CHERRY VALLEY

Cherry Valley was the first settlement in Otsego County. Begun in 1739, it was long an outpost, the last point of civilization before reaching the Indian wilderness.

During the revolution, it was the place that the few settlers who were scattered throughout the county would come to when there was rumor of an Indian-tory march. Many of these pioneers were in the fort there when it was attacked on the morning of November 11, 1778. Some of the Cherry Valley residents, however, were outside the stockade and were surprised and killed on their run from their homes to the fort. Others were taken to Canada as prisoners.

AUCHINBRECK,
CHERRY VALLEY, N. Y.

AUCHINBRECK

Among those captured in the attack of 1778 were the children and the wife of Colonel Campbell, the owner of the cabin which stood on the sight of Auchinbreck, the later Campbell home. The cabin was burned in the raid, but the colonel escaped capture. After the revolution, the family was reunited and the home rebuilt.

William W. Campbell, the colonel's grandson, was a justice of the State Supreme Court. He resided here and wrote several pieces on the history of New York. Among these was the classic work, "Annals of Tryon County."

SOLDIERS BARRACKS 1862 CHERRY VALLEY, N.Y.

SOLDIERS BARRACKS

Otsego County is credited with enlisting 2,925 men to fight in the Civil War. Cherry Valley, where a National Guard Regiment had long been stationed, was particularly active in that conflict with fully one-tenth of its total population serving.

In 1870, an oblisk was erected in the village square to the memory of the forty-two Cherry Valley citizens who died in that war at the battles of second Bull Run, Petersburg, Gettysburg, Wilderness, Fredericksburg, Winchester, Antietam, and Cold Harbor.

The barracks in Cherry Valley quartered six hundred volunteers in the war's first four months.

Monument Square, Cherry Valley, N. Y.

MONUMENT SQUARE, CHERRY VALLEY

Cherry Valley was long a crossroads traversed by three sections of the great Western Turnpike. The first section extended from Albany to Cherry Valley; the second from Cherry Valley through Cooperstown and then west to Sherburne (mainly, the present Route 80). The third ran to Cazenovia (via Route 20).

In 1815, fifteen taverns catered to travelers within the village, and as many as forty praire schooners stopped for the night in the village square. In addition, there were other businesses: a marble works, a cabinetmaker, iron and brass foundries, tanneries, distilleries, hat and last factories as well as other industries and stores.

Main Street Looking up, Cherry Valley, N. Y.

MAIN ST. LOOKING UP, CHERRY VALLEY

The opening of the Erie Canal in 1825 took away much of the traffic on the Great Western Turnpike, and business in Cherry Valley declined. Another blow was the country's financial panic of 1837 which caused the failure of every merchant in the village. When the New York Central Railroad opened, more business was lost to the growing cities of the Mohawk Valley. The village received a boost when a railroad was built that connected it with Cobleskill and Albany, but it never again achieved the importance of those pre-canal days. In the twentieth century, the new Route 20 bypassed the village, and its final days on a main road were ended.

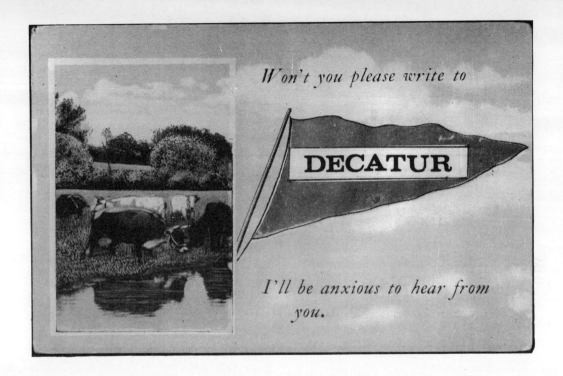

Won't you please write to

DECATUR

I'll be anxious to hear from you.

TOWN OF DECATUR

The smallest township in the county, with 12,841 acres, tiny Decatur has had a claim to fame. Lewis E. Waterman was born there in 1837. When he was sixteen, he moved west as did many others during the years just before the Civil War. But Mr. Waterman later returned to the Northeast, and in 1884, while living in New York City, he invented the first practicable fountain pen and founded the Waterman Pen Company.

100

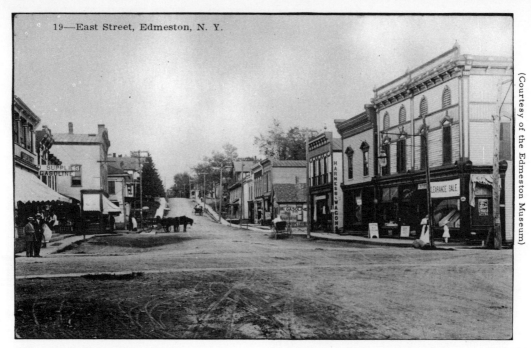

19—East Street, Edmeston, N. Y.

(Courtesy of the Edmeston Museum)

EAST STREET, EDMESTON

Edmeston is named for the British officer who was given the land in 1770. Colonel Edmeston never visited his property, but he did send Percifer Carr to settle the tract.

Mr. Carr came over from England with his wife, and they struggled to clear land and build a farm in the isolated territory. When the war broke out, Carr took the side of the British and helped the Tories. Because of this, the Oneidas, who sided with the Revolutionists, burnt his buildings and took him and his wife to Canada as their prisoner.

The Carrs returned after the Revolution and rebuilt only to be evicted by the colonel's heirs.

COLLAPSE OF DONKE'S BARBER SHOP MORNING AFTER THE EDMESTON FLOOD, SEPT. 3, 1905.

EDMESTON FLOOD

A disastrous flood struck Edmeston on September 3, 1905. Heavy rains swelled Mill Creek which runs through the center of the village. The village's two dams which were erected to power small industries were swept away carrying the livestock and the ruins of five barns down to the bridge at the village center. The wreckage there blocked the water creating a pond four feet deep in the business section.

The building pictured was built across the creek and, undermined by the flood, tumbled into the water. The large elm tree behind the building kept it from being washed down the stream.

No. 16-O. & W. Station, Edmeston, N. Y.

(Courtesy of Edmeston Museum)

O. & W. STATION, EDMESTON

The Wharton Valley Railroad was a seven mile extension, from New Berlin to Edmeston, of the New York, Ontario & Western.

Construction of the road began in August of 1888. One hundred Italian workmen labored on the grading which required much fill through the swamps of Pittsfield. But work progressed quickly, and railroad service started the following year.

The O & W, or the "Old & Weary" as it was nicknamed, hobbled along in shaky financial condition all of its life and finally went out of business in 1957.

(Courtesy of the Edmeston Museum)

STREET SCENE, SOUTH EDMESTON

Years ago, before the days of bulk tanks or even chest coolers, the product from the evening's milking was cooled in cans left overnight in spring water. Early in the morning, the farmer would milk again, and the total milk from the two milkings would be hauled by wagon to the milk depot. Here the contents would be weighed and processed at the local creamery or shipped raw on the milk train to New York City.

Farms were smaller then, and the average yield per farm per day would be about four or five forty pound cans.

The street scene pictured in the card is in front of Page's store.

WEST EDMESTON, N.Y.

WEST EDMESTON DAM

It has only been recently that communities have relied so extensively on large, faraway corporations to supply the energy needed for lighting and machinery. Before, many tiny local enterprises filled the need.

The village of West Edmeston was one of the first small villages to have electric power (supplied by the water power from the Unadilla River). As in other places, the electricity would be used only for lighting and not available during the daylight hours. Later, when more power was available, it was supplied on a schedule to suit local needs: Monday forenoons for washing, Tuesday for ironing, Friday for vacuuming.

South Street, West Exeter, N. Y.

SOUTH STREET, WEST EXETER

One of the first settlers of the town of Exeter was the Englishman John Tunnicliff who came there just prior to the Revolution. After a short time, he left to visit England. But before he left, he buried 2,000 English soverigns, the family silver, and some tools on his property.

It was a number of years before he could return, and when he did he found the area so grown wild that he could not locate his cache. Years later, the tools were found, but the whereabouts of the treasure remains a mystery.

Visible in this view are the general store, the Methodist Church, and the Matteson home (Matteson's Mills was the village's old name.).

Main Street, Schuyler Lake, N. Y.

MAIN STREET, SCHUYLER LAKE

This view of Main Street, Schuyler Lake shows the porches of two inns which were built in the first part of the nineteenth century. The first, the Schuyler Lake Hotel, is still standing. The second, the Bullion House, was torn down in 1959.

Inns of the early 1800's sheltered the drovers and other travelers who journeyed on the roads and turnpikes in the days before the canals and railroads. Later, they catered to the vacationers who came from the cities to spend the hot months in the countryside near the lake.

Trolley View, Oneonta and Mohawk Valley Trolley.

TROLLEY VIEW, SCHUYLER LAKE

Just north of the village of Schuyler Lake, the trolley crossed over Oaks Creek to run up the east side of Canadarago Lake.

In its heyday, the trolley company had a parlor car, the Otsego, which ran daily trips between Utica and Oneonta. The car had an observation platform enclosed with highly polished brass rails. Inside, there were fine wicker chairs, carpeting, and curtains. The passengers were cared for by a courteous porter who wore a white uniform in the summer and a blue one the rest of the year.

The Otsego carried many notable people, but perhaps the most famous was Teddy Roosevelt.

MAIN ST., HARTWICK, N.Y. 404.

SUPERVISORS HOME BANK STORE

MAIN STREET, HARTWICK

John Christopher Hartwick was a native German who was ordained a Lutheran minister in London in 1745 and then came to America. He served the Palatine congregation along the Hudson and there met many Indians from whom he bought a large tract of land along the Susquehanna.

Rev. Hartwick roamed the Central New York area preaching to the settlers and Indians. It was his plan to establish on his property a colony set up according to his idea of truly Christian principles and to use it to convert the Indians. His dream was never realized, but Hartwick Seminary (and later the college) was founded with his wish for a religious institute in mind.

East Main Street, Hartwick, N. Y.

EAST MAIN STREET, HARTWICK

When gold was discovered in California in 1848, the citizens of Otsego County were not immune to the gold fever that took hold of the country. Many individuals throughout the county got together to travel to the new gold fields near Sacramento. One such party of eight was headed by Frederick T. Jarvis of Hartwick. The group left in a lumber wagon drawn by four horses with "Bound for California" painted on the side. They eventually made it to New York where six of the party continued the journey by ship. Jarvis returned to Hartwick fourteen months later. The whole adventure netted him a $200 loss.

110

Bird's—Eye View of Hartwick, N. Y.

BIRDSEYE VIEW OF HARTWICK

The village of Hartwick was once the headquarters of the old trolley line between Oneonta and Herkimer. The electric power house was located here to provide power for the line before the Colliersville plant was built. The car barns for repair and housing of most of the rolling stock were also here.

The Employees Mutual Benefit Association of the railroad opened its "Tammany Hall" clubhouse in Hartwick in 1917.

Trolley View near Hartwick, N. Y.

TROLLEY VIEW NEAR HARTWICK

The scene pictured here is a serene one of a little trolley car rounding a wooded bend, but the times of the Southern New York were not always peaceful, particularly during the building of the road. Workers blocked the rails for two weeks outside Richfield Springs when their pay was held up for a month. Another wage dispute resulted in a battle along the line south of Hartwick which ended in a worker being shot dead by company officials backed by police.

When the line was to be hooked up with another extending to Herkimer from Mohawk, the citizens of the latter village rioted to keep the terminus there, and martial law was declared.

Main St. Looking North, Laurens, N. Y.

MAIN ST. AND DEPOT, LAURENS

Italian laborers provided the work force for the building of the trolley line which reached Laurens on July 4, 1901. During the celebration picnic that day, they entertained the townsfolk by singing selections from Italian operas. To many, this was their first exposure to classical music.

As in other towns, the coming of the trolley brought people out of the isolation of their little villages and brought them in contact with the broader, changing world. It also aided commerce. The quick, efficient transportation spurred the growth of dairies and made liquid milk a staple of even the city dweller's diet.

4416 ENTRANCE TO OTSEGO PARK, ONEONTA, N. Y.
PUBL. BY ONEONTA DEP'T STORE.

OTSEGO PARK, LAURENS

This amusement center located between West Oneonta and the village of Laurens was operated by the trolley company.

Leaving the trolley and entering the area over a wooden bridge which spanned Otego Creek, the visitor entered a wooded area which contained a concession stand and picnic tables.

The park was closed in 1906 when the railroad's larger park opened on the east side of Canandaraga Lake. A farmer then tore down the wooden walkway and used the area as a pasture.

Main Street, Laurens, N. Y.

PEET'S STORE, MAIN ST., LAURENS

Built in the 1820's as a general store, the building in foreground of the picture is still standing. David Peet bought the business toward the end of that century and added to it. Besides serving the usual general store functions, the store also sold coal, rented bicycles, and manufactured tin butter pails. Mr. Peet also served as the telegraph operator in the village.

The next store east was moved there from another location in the village and served as a jewelry store and a photographer's studio.

Laurens High School.

LAURENS HIGH SCHOOL

Old timers frequently tell of the hard times they had as students in the old days. But the lot of the teacher was also apparently not an easy one. Aside from the main task of teaching a room full of students of various grade levels and abilities, teachers had to perform the various everyday duties of sweeping and dusting, filling the school's lamps and cleaning their chimneys and wicks, hauling water, and carrying enough coal to keep the stove hot through the day's session.

After ten hours in school, it was recommended that the teacher "should spend the remaining time reading the Bible or other good books."

The Bobbin and Acid Factory, Maryland, N. Y.

BOBBIN AND ACID FACTORY, MARYLAND

The town of Maryland has had a number of industries which used the railroad to ship their various products. There was the Bobbin and Acid factory at the village of Maryland which used the products of the surrounding forests.

In Schenevus there was a tannery which also used hemlock bark to process 14,000 hides a year. The village also had the Sash and Blind Manufactory, a grist mill, and a feed and plaster mill which made 200 tons of plaster a year.

HOTEL SILVER, SCHENEVUS

Originally called Jacksonboro, the village received its current name from the creek running through it. The origin of the word "Schenevus" is not clear. One authority states that the Indian word means "speckled fish," while another claims it was the name of an Indian who lived there around the time the first white settlers came to the county.

Main Street, Looking West, Schenevus, N. Y.

MAIN STREET, SCHENEVUS

Notice the crosswalk spanning the street in front of the barber shop. Such walkways can be seen in many old cards and photos. Made of wood planks or of gravel, they were needed by the pedestrians in crossing the unpaved roads.

Dusty during dry spells, ankle deep in mud when it rained or thawed, few roads were surfaced until the beginning of this century when automobile travel came into vogue. And in the winter, snow was left on the roads to be packed down by the traffic of horses and sleds.

D. & H. Station, Schenevus, N. Y.

D. & H. STATION, SCHENEVUS

When the Albany & Susquehanna came to Schenevus in the summer of 1865, the town celebrated. The railroad sent a special train with
a sleek new wood-burning locomotive pulling
a string of wooden cars freshly painted a bright
yellow. Townspeople were invited aboard to
inspect the train. There they were impressed
by the red plush seats, polished overhead oil
lamps, and small stoves at each end of the cars.

The A&S was later sold to the Delaware &
Hudson in order to avoid being taken over by
the robber baron Jay Gould.

Annual Fishing Carnival, Schenevus, N. Y., "The Fish are Coming."

ICE FISHING, SCHENEVUS

Fishing parties were once common in Otsego County during the winter months. People gathered together to cut a long trench in the ice across a river or stream. Half of the party would then go up stream and pound on the ice with axes or bars to drive the fish down to the trench where the other members of the party waited with spears or nets to land them.

Similar parties were organized by companies, railroads, or communities to cut and harvest enough blocks of ice to last an entire year.

Fishing Party, Schenevus Creek, 1,250 Fish, Wt. 1 Ton.

122

HIGH SCHOOL BUILDING, SCHENEVUS

The following are some of the guidelines set
by the state for teachers in 1872:

"Men teachers may take one evening a week
for courting purposes, or two evenings a week
if they attend church regularly.

"Women teachers who marry or engage in
unseemly conduct will be dismissed.

"Each teacher who smokes, uses liquor in
any form, frequents pool or public halls, or
gets shaved in a barber shop, will give good
reason to suspect his worth, intentions, in-
tegrity and honesty."

After five years of keeping to the rules, the
teacher could expect his weekly pay to raise 25¢.

BIRDS EYE VIEW MIDDLEFIELD, N.Y. 62.

BIRDSEYE VIEW OF MIDDLEFIELD

In the very early days of Otsego County, Middlefield was one of the most important settlements, and the residents pushed to have the county seat established in their town just as the citizens of Cherry Valley wanted it there. On this subject, Judge Cooper playfully remarked that the courthouse should be placed in Cooperstown, the jail in New-Town-Martin (as Middlefield was then called), and the gallows in Cherry Valley.

In Middlefield, as in the rest of the county, agriculture has always been the most important industry, but the town has also had two factories: a last factory and the Phoenix Woolen Mill.

WEST MAIN STREET, MILFORD, N. Y.

WEST MAIN STREET, MILFORD

The town of Milford (or "Suffrage," as it was initially called) was one of the first settled after the Revolution. The pioneers nearly starved to death the first year. Food was so scarce that by spring their diet consisted solely of wild leeks and milk. It was reported that because of the quantity of leeks eaten, you could smell a settler from a considerable distance. This situation persisted for six weeks until the still unripe wheat crop had advanced enough to be boiled and digested. That summer, seven bushels of corn would buy a yoke of oxen.

West Main Street, Milford, N. Y.

MAIN STREET, MILFORD

Milford was the town in which the county's powerful Wilber family got its start. David Wilber was a hops merchant here when he opened a private bank as a convenience in buying and selling that product.

In 1873, he opened a branch of that bank in Oneonta and later, with his son George, went from hops to public banking and a multitude of other financial enterprises.

Dam across Susquehanna River, Near Colliersville, N. Y.
32 feet high, forms a deep Lake many miles long

GOODYEAR LAKE DAM, COLLIERSVILLE

The dam and hydro-electric plant at Colliers-ville were built in 1907 by the trolley company to supplement a steam power plant at Hartwick. Besides powering the railway, electricity was also sold to homes and industries along the right of way.

The dam is thirty-six feet high and is of a hollow design that uses nineteen transverse triangular buttresses covered with a thin skin of concrete.

When construction of the dam was completed and the gates closed, it took just six days and two hours for the area to fill and create a two mile long, 520 acre lake.

Goodyear's Lake Dam, near Oneonta, N.Y.

12436

Old Wooden Bridge, Oneonta, N. Y.

COVERED BRIDGE, COLLIERSVILLE

In 1832, Captain Edward Thorn built a covered bridge along the present Route 7 just above Colliersville. It was constructed of hemlock timbers measuring three inches by ten inches. These were sawed at the nearby Goodyear sawmill and hauled to the site by oxen.

The bridge, the last one in use over the Susquehanna, was removed in 1929.

It is pleasant to think that covered bridges were sometimes referred to as "kissing bridges."

Below the Dam,
Portlandville, N.Y.

F. F. Townsend & family woole & nund gan of
him

PORTLANDVILLE DAM

The town of Milford got started in 1772 when
Mathew Cull came down from Cherry Valley
in search of a place where the river was shallow and swift and a good location for a mill.
And the village of Portlandville started with
a dam built across the river in 1814. This provided power for a sawmill on the east side and
a gristmill and woolen mill on the west side.

Until the Erie Canal was built, the sawmill
floated thousands of board feet of lumber down
the river on rafts to Baltimore. And throughout the nineteenth century, the clothing mills
were expanded and employed many men and
women.

Birds Eye View, Morris, N. Y.

BIRD'S-EYE VIEW, MORRIS

The first settlers in the village of Morris were French royalists who fled the French Revolution. Being supporters of the king, they named their community in honor of the beheaded Louis XVI and called the place Louisville.

But the first settlers in the township were a group of Baptists who settled north of the village in 1773. During the Revolution, they were first bullied by the British and then imprisoned by the Revolutionists. Finally, Oneida Indians burned their homes and took many of the peaceful group to Canada as prisoners of war.

WEST MAIN STREET, Morris, N. Y.

WEST MAIN STREET, MORRIS

The stone building on the southeast corner of Main and Broad Streets (now the First National Bank) was probably built along with the street's other native stone buildings in the 1830's. At various times it had been a grocery store, a hardware store, a hat shop, a harness shop, and a shoe store. A furniture and art store as well as an early telephone central office were once located in the rear.

The taller building next down the street, the Perry Block, contained three stores on ground level, living flats on the second floor, and two halls on the third. A pool room and a resturant were once located in the building.

Kenyon House, Morris, N. Y.

KENYON HOUSE, MORRIS

Built to replace an older hotel which burnt in 1883, the Kenyon House was a proud establishment in its day and hailed as a model of modern hotel building.

The owner of the hotel during this period, James P. Kenyon, was a very prominent person in Morris. He was one of those nineteenth century men of humble beginnings who came to own almost an entire town. Mr. Kenyon started out as a tailor and worked his way up to owning a wagon building business, a drug and grocery store and many of the structures on Main Street. He was president of the bank for seventeen years and owned the building it was and is housed in.

Hargrave Lake, Morris, N. Y.

Photo only copyrighted 1907 by N. W. Carey

HARGRAVE LAKE, MORRIS

Holman Harry Linn was a showman who headed a small circus which traveled throughout New England and New York. He bought one of the first automobiles and improved it to pull his wagons. Stumbling into Morris by chance in 1912, he saw the fairgrounds as a good place to winter the troupe, so he stayed, tinkered, thought, and soon had started a factory powered by the water of Hargrave Lake and the money of local backers. The unique, caterpillar-tread machines built there were sold all over the world, and the company prospered.

Linn later invented a one-wheel, automobile trailer and started a plant in Oneonta.

101—Morris Manor, near Gilbertsville, N. Y.

MORRIS MANOR, MORRIS

In 1776, while Lewis Morris was away in Philadelphia signing the Declaration of Independence, British troops raided his estate near New York City, burned his timber, took his cattle and horses, and chased off his family. When the Revolution was over, the newly formed government took Butternut Valley land which had been owned by his Tory brother and gave it to him as indemnification. Lewis never visited the land, but his son, Jacob, came here in 1787 and settled. The Manor was built in 1808 and is still occupied by the Morris family.

HANNAH COOPER MONUMENT, MORRIS

Hannah Cooper, sister of the novelist and daughter of the founder of Cooperstown, was killed at this spot (on Route 51) in 1800 when she was thrown from a horse while on her way to visit the Morris sisters at the old Manor.

The twenty-three year old woman was said to have been beautiful, lively, and good. She had many admirers among the nobility of the time, and her social sphere extended through the Northeast. One admirer erected this stone; another is buried next to her in Cooperstown; still another made sad pilgrimages to the spot where she died. This latter admirer was the young army lieutenant William Henry Harrison.

Baker Block, Garrettsville, N.Y.

GARRETTSVILLE, TOWN OF NEW LISBON

The village of Garretsville was long a center for the town's agricultural activity. One hundred years ago, that agriculture was different from today. There were many smaller farms then, and their products were of a greater variety. There were the usual dairy products and acres of land devoted to feeding cattle. But other crops were produced that are rarely seen in the county now. For instance, in 1874 the town yielded 3,077 bushels of buckwheat, 37,286 pounds of hops, 33,901 bushels of potatoes, 23,819 bushels of apples, 676 barrels of cider, and 73,260 pounds of maple sugar. That same year, there were 2,321 sheep shorn and 403 hogs slaughtered.

Free Baptist Church and Parsonage West Oneonta. N.Y.

FREE BAPTIST CHURCH, WEST ONEONTA

The first Free Will Baptist Church was located on Oneida Street in 1840. The wooden building was later moved, piece by piece, to the West Oneonta site of the present church. Later, it was moved next to the hotel which stood on the present property of the Reinhardt-Andrus Company. The brick building shown here was erected in 1907. Sixteen years later the church merged with the First Baptist to create the West Oneonta Baptist Church.

Notice the shed beside the church where the horses of the church members were sheltered while services were in progress.

Hop Picking - Oneonta, Otsego Co. N.Y.

HOP PICKING

During most of the nineteenth century, central
New York was by far the leading hop producing
area in the country, and from Otsego County
came nearly one third of the country's harvest.
With the opening of the West as a grain producing region, however, the area lost its importance. And when the blue mold disease hit at
the end of the century, the industry died.

Hops were grown on vines which climbed
cords attached to high poles. In September,
the plants were harvested by cutting the vines
and then hand-picking the hops. Besides the
work of harvesting, much labor was needed for
cutting and arranging the poles and in pruning.

Main St., OTEGO, N. Y.

MAIN STREET, OTEGO

The Indian place names of Otsego County are either Algonquin or Iroquois. The natives were not very specific or consistent in what they called areas, and frequently, a place received many different names, and none of these needed to be related to a significant characteristic or event. It was the early pioneers and surveyors who needed to take the naming game more seriously, although even they were not always so exact in their rendering of Indian words. Hence, "Otego" is given at various times as Wauteghe, Atega, Adiga, Odego, Otage, Otago, and Adige.

The village of Otego has also had the non-Indian names of Hamburg and Huntsville.

M. E. Church and Parsonage, OTEGO, N. Y.

M. E. CHURCH AND PARSONAGE, OTEGO

The cost of constructing the Methodist Episcopal Church back in 1852 was $1,125.

At services back in those days, the men sat on one side of the choir; the women on the other.

There was no organ, and the congregation tuned up for singing with a tuning fork. During the singing and the long sermons, the sexton went about snuffing and relighting the chandeliers' tallow candles and putting more fuel in the wood stove.

Post office and Susquehanna House,
OTEGO, N.Y.

POST OFFICE AND SUSQUEHANNA HOUSE

The Susquehanna House, which stood on the site that the elementary school now occupies, was originally a private residence of T. R. Austin. A merchant and entrepreneur, Mr. Austin seems to have been a curious man. Of French descent, he was known for his aristocratic manner and fancy dress. He is said to have been on Fulton's steamboat on its maiden voyage up the Hudson. He had a brother who later lived with him whose background was shrouded in mystery but seems at one time to have been a privateersman on board a ship called The True Blooded Yankee.

In 1852, Austin, an old man then, set off to relocate in Wisconsin but died in Unadilla.

RANDALLS MILL DAM

FLYCREEK

M.E. CHURCH

THE POND BLISS ESTATE

GREETINGS FROM FLYCREEK, N.Y.

FLY CREEK, TOWN OF OTSEGO

The village, of course, gets its name from the stream passing through it. But the creek is not named after a type of insect. "Fly" is merely a corruption of "vlei" which itself is either an Indian word or a contraction of the Dutch "vallei," meaning a shallow morass on a hill.

During the first half of the nineteenth century, Fly Creek was an important tool manufacturing center and one of the most prosperous communities in the county. At that time, it also had a wire factory and a pail factory.

Main Street, Fly Creek, N.Y.

MAIN STREET, FLY CREEK

One of the town of Otsego's most famous off-spring was Erastus F. Beadle, the father of the "dime novel." Starting his career as an apprentice at Phinney's printshop in Coopers-town, Beadle later moved to Buffalo and began to publish on his own. One item, "The Dime Song Book," opened up a line of song, joke, and sport books which led to biographies and then to fiction and adventure. These books were sold at camps during the Civil War and were the very successful forerunners of both comic books and the mass-market paperbacks of today.

The above card shows the main crossroads of Fly Creek with its hotel and stores.

13—East Main Street Bridge, Fly Creek, N. Y.

EAST MAIN STREET BRIDGE, FLY CREEK

David Shipman, the "Leatherstocking" or "Natty Bumpo" of the famous novels, was a resident of the town of Otsego who lived in a log cabin on the east bank of Oaks Creek between Toddsville and Fly Creek. He is said to have dressed in tanned deerskin and carried a very long rifle. Known in the area as a great hunter, Shipman spent his time roaming the forests with his dogs. Legend has it that he died in Otsego and is buried somewhere in the town in an unmarked grave.

Old Stone Mill at Index, near Cooperstown N. Y.

MILL AT INDEX, TOWN OF OTSEGO

This was one of ten cotton mills which were built in Otsego County in the first half of the nineteenth century. The county's abundant water power made them possible.

The Hope Factory in Index received its water from Oaks Creek via a half mile ditch. The mill itself was built in 1824 on the site of a wooden one that was constructed fifteen years before.

Cotton was brought up the Hudson River in ships from the South and then transported in wagons or sleds over the turnpikes to the mills where it was woven into cloth.

The mill's main building was razed in 1931 and its stone used in the Fenimore House.

VIEW FROM HOTEL OAKESVILLE N.Y.

OAKSVILLE, TOWN OF OTSEGO

Oaksville was once an industrial village with
a large cotton mill as well as smaller industries
that used the creek for power and the turnpike
for transporting their products.

The rest of the county also had its industry.
Indeed, in 1835 Otsego County had seventy gristmills, nearly five hundred sawmills, and many
carding and fulling mills to prepare yarn from
flax. There were ten cotton mills, and two
woolen mills handled much of the wool from
the county's 400,000 sheep. There was also a
papermill, six iron works, a brass foundry,
fifteen distilleries, a brewery, two piano and
organ factories, a hat factory, and a comb plant.

Hoboken Dam

HOBOKEN DAM, PITTSFIELD

Throughout the nineteenth century, small industry still produced nearly everything. And among the very small plants of Otsego County, cheap and readily available water power was the common source of energy. Not only gristmills and sawmills were water-powered, but textile mills, papermills, furniture factories, foundries, and many more industries depended upon dams thrown up on rivers and streams.

The Hoboken Dam on Wharton Creek in Pittsfield raised the water to flow through a canal to the Borden's Condensery three-quarters of a mile away. There the water fell approximately twenty feet onto a horizontal wheel.

Largest Condensery in the World, New Berlin, N.Y.

BORDEN'S CONDENSERY, PITTSFIELD

Until the 1860's, the only method of preserving milk was to make it into cheese. It was then that a Chenango County native Gail Borden invented a condensed milk process that made him rich and gave birth to a huge food corporation. Around the the turn of the century, that company's big-

gest plant, and the world's largest condensery, stood not far from the Unadilla River in the town of Pittsfield.

The plant used some of the buildings of the old Arkwright Cotton Factory that was erected on that site in 1832. All that now remains of either plant is a section of concrete flooring.

GREETING FROM UNADILLA FORKS N.Y.

COPYRIGHT 1906 BY H.M. BEACH

UNADILLA FORKS, PLAINFIELD

Located in the northwest corner of the county, the town of Plainfield is now exclusively a farming area. But once, like all of the other towns in Otsego, it had mills that made use of the plentiful water power.

Unadilla Forks has always been the largest community in the township, but Plainfield Center also had a healthy population. The hamlet had long been a Welsh community, and even toward the beginning of the twentieth century, church services there were still conducted in the Welsh language.

Richfield Springs, N.Y. The "Earlington".

EARLINGTON, RICHFIELD SPRINGS

The Iroquois were the first to use Richfield's mineral springs. Here they treated frostbite and illnesses of the skin and bone. Dr. Horace Manley erected the first bathhouse in 1821 and administered the "water cure" to his patients. But the real lush days for Richfield Springs began in 1871 when the Lackawana Railroad spur reached the village. The health center then became a resort for summertime pleasure.

BATH HOUSE, RICHFIELD SPRINGS, N. Y.

BATH HOUSE, RICHFIELD SPRINGS

The large hotels were located near what is now the village park. The Bath House pictured here was on the rear grounds of that park, and the Earlington was across Main Street. It had large grounds in the back complete with a sizable bicycle track.

Three thousand people came each summer, and many of these visitors remained the whole season. Some of the more famous guests who have spent "the heated term" at Richfield Springs are Thomas Edison, Cyrus McCormick, Admiral George Dewey, Sarah Orne Jewett, and Oscar Wilde.

The Berkeley-Waiontha, Richfield Springs, N. Y.

BERKELEY-WAIONTHA, RICHFIELD SPRINGS

The Berkeley-Waiontha Hotel was a favorite of wealthy Latin American visitors. During August of 1919, 135 Cubans had stayed there. And there was much for the guests to do. The area offered recreation in golf, tennis, polo, roller-skating, and horseback riding. An auto-mobile hill climbing contest was an annual event.

The first summer theatre at a resort area was held in the village in 1886. Orchestral concerts performed by some of the best musicians in the country were given twice daily, and formal balls and informal hops were held regularly.

Another very popular amusement was a parade of coaches complete with liveried coachmen.

Richfield Springs, N.Y.   High School Building.

HIGH SCHOOL, RICHFIELD SPRINGS

When opened in 1886, Richfield Springs High School was thought to be the finest in central New York. Designed by Worthy Niver of Fultonville, the building boasted a large assembly hall in the roofed area of the third floor.

There were eight teachers employed when the first 250 students began classes.

The building was demolished in 1939, and all the brick and stonework (including the sealed cornerstone) was used as fill on a lot on Center Street.

The old high school site, on Bonner Street between Park and Center, is now a trailer park.

A View of Canandaraga Lake.

A VIEW OF CANANDARAGA LAKE

Deowongo Island is a wooded body of land about four acres in size near the east side of Canandaraga Lake. Archaeological expeditions there have turned up much evidence of Indian inhabitation. Refuse mounds and the foundation poles of an Iroquois longhouse were discovered near the northern tip of the island, and the eastern shore of the lake is dotted with Indian burial grounds.

Just before the first New Englanders came to settle the area during the last years of the eighteenth century, a group of French trappers and their Indian wives lived on the lake. Their cabins stood near the Lake House.

Lake House on Canadarago Lake, Richfield Springs, N. Y.

LAKE HOUSE, RICHFIELD

The Lake House (still in operation as a resturant) was built in 1843 to cater to the visitors of the spring. Renowned for its cuisine, it was a frequent stopping point of the carriage parade from the village. The inn also catered to hunters and fishermen. Also, the grounds contained a roller-skating rink and an open dance pavilion on the lake shore. The steamboat T. R. Proctor took visitors from its dock on excursions around Canandaraga Lake.

During Prohibition, the Lake House was a popular speak-easy and was used as a summer residence by Jack "Legs" Diamond.

View from McCredy's, on the trolley line to Richfield Springs, N. Y.   a.W.

TROLLEY LINE TO RICHFIELD SPRINGS

The success of the electric railway system in the county can be determined from a few facts. At one time the Southern New York had fourteen round trip passenger runs daily between Oneonta and Mohawk and eighteen between Coop- erstown and the juction at Index. In addition, there were many freight and milk runs so that a total of 109 trains operated daily over the seventy miles of track.

Special excursions were run to an amuse- ment park the company built on the east side of Canandaraga Lake in Richfield.

Roseboom N.Y.

ROSEBOOM

Like many of the county's towns, Roseboom was once a more active place than at present. The town's current population of approximately five hundred is less than one-third of the number of one hundred years ago.

In 1872, the village alone had a post office, two churches, two stores, a hotel, a gristmill, two sawmills, a planing mill, two blacksmith shops, a cheese factory, a shoe shop, a millinery and dressmaking shop, and a doctor's office.

A temperance newspaper, "The Temperance Canoe," was published monthly in Roseboom. Its motto: "Fear God and Paddle Your Own Canoe."

Springfield Center, N. Y.

(Town Hall)

No. 4009. Publ. Atlas Society, New York. Made in Germany.

TOWN HALL, SPRINGFIELD CENTER

Springfield has long been a crossroads town. Perhaps the first road in Otsego County was the trail cut by the Dutch pioneers who came to Springfield from Canajoharie ten years before the Revolution. And it was this same road that General Clinton's men improved and tra-veled on in 1779. The branch that goes down to Hyde Bay had long been referred to as the Continental Road (after the Continental Army).

The Third Great Western Turnpike (1809) came through Springfield.

The Otsego Lake Turnpike of 1825 and the later Fort Plain and Cooperstown Plankroad were attempts at improving transportation.

EAST SPRINGFIELD, N.Y., OLD ACADEMY

OLD ACADEMY, EAST SPRINGFIELD

When the Revolution broke out, many of the settlers of Springfield went to fight in the militia. One such soldier was Captain Thomas Davy of Springfield who, at the battle of Oriskany, was shot from his horse and killed. Captain Davy's wife learned of her husband's fate when his familiar white horse wandered riderless back to its home.

Mrs. Davy's house was later burned by the Tories and Indians when they destroyed the settlements in 1777. She escaped capture by hiding in the woods with her child shielded beneath her skirts.

The pictured Academy dates from the 1860's.

UNADILLA, N. Y.   Unadilla from Evergreen Hill.

UNADILLA

During the first quarter of the nineteenth century, Unadilla was the most important town in the southern half of Otsego County. This was due to its being the western terminus of the Catskill Turnpike and the eastern terminus of the Ithaca-Susquehanna Turnpike. In those days, if you wanted to reach any point in the newly settled central or southwestern part of the state, you crossed the Susquehanna on Wattles' Ferry (or, later, over the river on the covered bridge) and stopped at the inn in Unadilla.

When the Erie Canal was built, however, most of the traffic took that route, and the new settlers preferred the country serviced by the canal.

UNADILLA, N. Y.   Main Street

MAIN STREET, UNADILLA

When we think of an Otsego County writer, we think, of course, of James Fenimore Cooper. But Otsego has had other important authors. The novelist's daughter, Susan Cooper, was an author in her own right. Willard Huntington Wright lived for a time in Oneonta and wrote his first novel, "A Man of Promise," using that city as its locale. His later detective novels, written under the name S. S. VanDine, won him much fame in the 1920's.

Unadilla's own Francis Whiting Halsey was a respected writer on the subjects of art, travel, and New York State history. He was also the first editor of the New York Times Book Review.

WELLSBRIDGE, N. Y.   Birdseye View

WELLS BRIDGE, TOWN OF UNADILLA

The town of Unadilla is bordered by two rivers: the Unadilla River on the west (which also formed the border of Indian territory according to the 1768 treaty) and the Susquehanna on the south. The latter river was frequently used for trans-ferring logs and lumber via rafts that rode the high water in spring. Later, the railroads transported nearly all of the county's produce from a number of points. The village of Wells Bridge has been a station for both methods of transportation.

Westville, N.Y.

WESTVILLE, TOWN OF WESTFORD

Westford is one of the county's towns whose population peaked over a hundred years ago when the total was nearly four times the present 450. Still, Westford has had notable citizens and has participated in the larger affairs of the country. When the Civil War started, Westford's sons went off to fight, and they faired much worse than most. Of the thirty who are recorded as having enlisted from that town, nine are known to have been killed, and five more were wounded.

Andrew S. Draper, a native of Westford, a-chieved prominence as president of the University of Illinois and the first Commissioner of Education in the State of New York (1904-1913).

Central Hotel

MAIN STREET, WORCESTER, N. Y.

MAIN STREET, WORCESTER

One of the first pioneers to come to Worcester was Solomon Garfield from Westminister, Worcester Co., Mass. He and his wife, Sally, and their children came here in 1790 and settled in the eastern part of the village. Their grandson Abram was born in Worcester but left in 1820 for Ohio to become a pioneer there. His son was James A. Garfield, our twentieth president.

A number of the president's ancestors are buried in Worcester. Among them is James' grandfather, Thomas, who died of smallpox in 1801 and was buried in the village's first burying ground at the Main and Decatur corner.

Central Hotel
Worcester, N.Y. O.M. Sloan Prop.

CENTRAL HOTEL, WORCESTER

There has been a tavern on the site of the Central (now the Worcester Inn) since 1818. But the building pictured was built in 1875.

About one hundred years ago, the hotel was a favorite stopping place for traveling salesmen. They came by train to the village, roomed at the hotel, and rented "rigs" from the establishment's livery stable to reach the communities in the area. The hotel even had a "sample room" in which the salesmen displayed their wares.

Later, the livery stable, located behind the building, became the village's first garage for the servicing of passing automobiles.

UNION SCHOOL. EAST WORCESTER, N.Y.

UNION SCHOOL, EAST WORCESTER

Through most of the nineteenth century, the curriculum in schools was primarily very basic, and education above the elementary level tended to be classical with courses in such subjects as Latin, Greek, and rhetoric. But toward the end of the century, the growing trend of nation-alism brought about the push of patiotism and the introduction of American History as a required subject. It was at this time that the law requiring the display of the flag in the classroom was introduced. Later, with the passage of the Compulsory Education Law (1906), practical courses were introduced.

The Union School (c. 1860-1915) was on Main.

Bibliography

AMERICAN REVOLUTION BICENTENNIAL.
Oneonta, NY, 1976

Bacon, Edwin F., OTSEGO COUNTY: GEO-
GRAPHICAL AND HISTORICAL. Oneonta,
NY: Oneonta Herald, 1902

Beers, F.W., ATLAS OF OTSEGO COUNTY.
New York, 1868

Bicentennial Committee of the Town of Oneonta,
ARROWHEADS, FENCES, AND IRON HORSES.
Oneonta, NY, 1976

Birdsall, Ralph, STORY OF COOPERSTOWN.
New York: Charles Scribner's Sons, 1925

Blakely, S.B., HISTORY OF OTEGO. Cooperstown, NY: Crist, Scott & Parshall, 1907

Burlington Bicentennial Committee, BURLING-
TON: THEN AND NOW. 1977

Butterfield, Roy L., IN OLD OTSEGO. Otsego
County Board of Supervisors, 1959

Child, Hamilton, GAZETTEER & BUSINESS
DIRECTORY OF OTSEGO CO. FOR 1872-
1873. Syracuse, NY, 1872

Cooper, J.F.; Shaw, S.M.; Littell, W.R.; Hollis,
H.H.; HISTORY OF COOPERSTOWN. Coop-
erstown, NY: New York State Historical
Association, 1976

Edmeston Museum, EDMESTON: ECHOES OF
THE PAST. (volumes I & II) Edmeston, NY,
1976 & 1978

Foote, Joyce, MORRIS, NEW YORK 1773-1923.
Morris, NY, 1970

Frost, James A., LIFE ON THE UPPER SUS-
QUEHANNA 1783-1860. New York: Colum-
bia University, 1951

Gray, Kate M., HISTORY OF SPRINGFIELD.
General James Clinton Chapter No. 640,
Daughters of the American Rev., 1935

Halsey, Francis W., OLD NEW YORK FRON-
TIER. New York: Scribners, 1901

Halsey, Francis W., PIONEERS OF UNADILLA
VILLAGE. Unadilla, NY, 1902

Hunt, Walter L., VILLAGE BEAUTIFUL. Unadilla, NY, 1957

Hurd, D. H., HISTORY OF OTSEGO COUNTY.
Philadelphia: Everts and Fariss, 1878

Jones, Louis C., COOPERSTOWN. Otsego Co.
Historical Society, 1957

Moore, Edwin R., IN OLD ONEONTA. 6 volumes,
Upper Susquehanna Historical Society and
the Village Printer, Laurens, 1962-1970

Myers, H. N., BICENTENNIAL HISTORY OF

OTEGO. Town Board, Otego, NY, 1976

Nestle, David F., LEATHERSTOCKING ROUTE. Oneonta, NY, 1959

Otsego County Council of Senior Citizens, HISTORICAL MEMORIES OF OTSEGO COUNTY. First and second editions, Opportunities for Otsego, Inc., 1975 and 1976

Schull, Diantha Dow, LANDMARKS OF OTSEGO COUNTY. Syracuse, NY: Syracuse University Press, 1980

SIGHTS IN ONEONTA. Glens Falls, NY: C.H. Possons, 1887

Slawson, A.F., Schull, D.S., ONEONTA LANDMARKS. Laurens, NY: Mid-State Recreations Publications, Inc., 1973

Streeter, Hilda E., HISTORIC CHERRY VALLEY. Cherry Valley Memorial Library, 1924

TOWN OF MIDDLEFIELD: SOME HISTORY NOTES GATHERED HERE AND THERE. 1961

Wardell, Bernice, HISTORY OF LAURENS TOWNSHIP. 1975

Weeks, Pearl A., HISTORY OF HARTWICK. Hartwick Reporter, 1934

Worcester History Committee, TOWN OF WORCESTER. c.1951

Acknowledgments

Edmeston Museum
Milne Library, Oneonta
Milton and Dorothy Moore, Pittsfield
NYSHA Library, Cooperstown
Mrs. Bernie Nonenmacher, Edmeston
Bobbi Nonenmacher, Edmeston
Virginia O'Connor, Pittsfield